MORRILL ELEMENTARY SCHOOL
34880000812086

W9-BBC-436

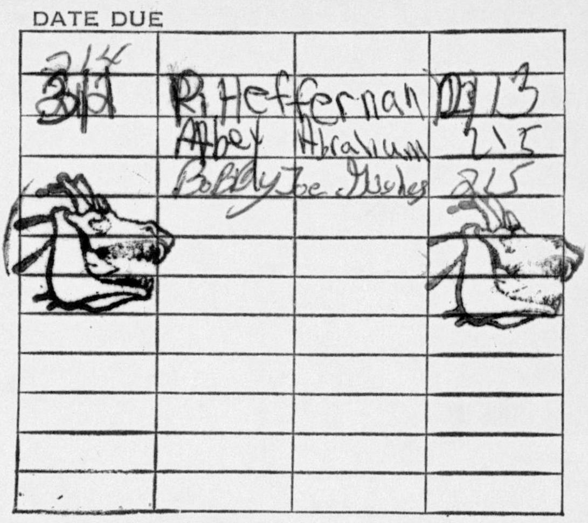
940.4
S
c.1
SNYDER
MILITARY HISTORY OF
THE LUSITANIA
DATE DUE

MORRILL SCHOOL

The MILITARY HISTORY of THE LUSITANIA

FRANKLIN WATTS, INC.
575 Lexington Avenue, New York 10022

THE MILITARY HISTORY of
THE LUSITANIA

by Louis L. Snyder

Library of Congress Catalog Card Number: 65-15077

Printed in the United States of America by
Polygraphic Company of America
2 3 4 5 6 7

This Book Is For
MARK ALLEN SNYDER

It is a deed for which a Hun would blush, a Turk be ashamed, and a Barbary pirate apologize. To speak of technicalities and the rules of war, in the face of such wholesale murder on the high seas, is a waste of time. . . . The torpedo that sank the Lusitania *also sank Germany in the opinion of mankind. . . . It is at once a crime and a monumental folly.*

— *New York* Nation, *May 13, 1915*

As far as the Lusitania *is concerned, it was not only our right but also our holy duty* (unsere heilige Pflicht) *to sink her if we had the chance. And no consideration for any light-headed passengers could have hindered us!*

— *Dr. Karl Bindung, Professor at the University of Leipzig, 1915*

Contents

The MILITARY HISTORY of THE LUSITANIA

Some survivors of the Lusitania. *United Press International*

"Sink the 'Lusitania'? Tommyrot!"

ON SATURDAY MORNING, May 1, 1915, *The New York Times* and other metropolitan newspapers carried the customary announcements of sailings on the Cunard Line:

CUNARD
Europe via Liverpool
LUSITANIA
Fastest and Largest Steamer
now in Atlantic Service sails

SATURDAY, May 1, 10 A.M.

Transylvania,	Fri., May 7, 5 P.M.
Orduna,	Tues., May 18, 10 A.M.
Tuscania,	Fri., May 21, 5 P.M.
LUSITANIA,	Sat., May 29, 10 A.M.
Transylvania,	Fri., June 4, 5 P.M.

Next to this advertisement appeared another conspicuous and certainly unusual notice:

ADVERTISEMENT.

NOTICE!

TRAVELLERS intending to embark on the Atlantic voyage are reminded that a state of war exists between Germany and her allies and Great Britain and her allies; that the zone of war includes the waters adjacent to the British Isles; that, in accordance with formal notice given by the Imperial German Government, vessels flying the flag of Great Britain, or of any of her allies, are liable to destruction in those waters and that travellers sailing in the war zone on ships of Great Britain or her allies do so at their own risk.

IMPERIAL GERMAN EMBASSY

WASHINGTON, D. C., APRIL 22, 1915.

The German government later claimed that it had given two previous warnings: *Warning No. 1*, made on February 4, 1915, some three months before the *Lusitania* disaster, when Germany announced that she would destroy all enemy ships found within a war zone around the British Isles; *Warning No. 2*, made indirectly but clearly by the sinking of dozens of merchantmen inside the war zone. Actually, Germany had destroyed sixty-six ships in the eleven weeks before she sank the *Lusitania*.

The newspaper advertisement placed by the Imperial German Embassy appeared on the very day the mammoth liner sailed from New York. Was this proof that the Germans had planned the sinking? The *Manchester Guardian* thought it was, for the *Lusitania* was the first transatlantic liner to be sunk in the war zone. Technically, the *Guardian* was correct. On March 28, 1915, the *Falaba*, a British passenger ship, had been torpedoed with a loss of 104 lives, including one American; but the *Falaba* was not, strictly speaking, a transatlantic liner — she had been bound for West Africa. At any rate, said the *Manchester Guardian*, it was clear that the sinking of the *Lusitania* was deliberate, and that the Germans intended to sink any ships — whether warships, freighters, or passenger liners — that ventured into the war zone from then on.

Two days after the *Lusitania* tragedy, Count Johann von Bernstorff, the German ambassador in Washington, said that he had received the warning notice from his government some time before, with orders to publish it. "Thinking it a great mistake," he said, "I threw it into a drawer of my desk and hoped that Berlin would forget about it." On the day before the *Lusitania*'s departure, he continued, he had received a wireless message from Berlin asking specifically whether he had received the notice, and whether he had published it, and, if he had not, ordering him to publish it at once. Von Bernstorff complied by sending the notice out as a paid advertisement to be inserted near the sailing notices of the steamship lines.

The warning was received both flippantly and seriously by American citizens. The Germans were bluffing, were they not? Would they really be foolish enough to destroy an unarmed vessel carrying women, children, and babies? Surely that advertisement was a joke, a silly performance below the dignity of a diplomatic representative of any government. Everybody knew that the *Lusitania* was so fast she could run away from any U-boat the Germans had. Sensible persons knew that the British Admiralty would see to it that the ship was protected when she arrived close to the Irish coast.

Someone went to Captain William Thomas Turner, master of the *Lusitania*, and called his attention to the newspaper warning. He laughed and said: "I wonder what the Germans will do next. Well, it doesn't seem as if they had scared many people from going on the ship by the look of the pier and passenger list."

Charles Klein, an American playwright, was among those who refused to be scared. Interviewed by a *New York Times* reporter before the ship sailed, Klein said that he was going to devote his time on the voyage to thinking about his new play, *Potash and Perlmutter in Society*, and would have no time to worry about trifles. Klein lost his life when the ship went down.

Another traveler, fifty-four-year-old Elbert Hubbard, famous as lecturer, author, and publisher, said he believed that the German Emperor had ordered the advertisement to be placed in the newspapers. He added jokingly that if he (Hubbard) were aboard the liner when she was torpedoed, he would denounce the Kaiser in his publication *The Philistine*. Hubbard lost his life before he could complete his denunciation.

People in general just did not take the warning seriously as the doomed liner sailed on schedule. It was unthinkable that the Germans would go so far as to sink an *unarmed passenger vessel*. The attitude of disbelief came through in a dispatch sent home on May 3, 1915, by the Washington correspondent of *The Times* of London, in which he stated that Americans were as safe on the *Lusitania* as they were on Broadway. The German warning, wrote the British journalist, was "a piece of impudent bluff," "an insolent attempt to prejudice British commerce," and "an infantile effort to make Americans afraid of the nonexistent."

There were other people, however, who took the warning seriously. At the Cunard dock in New York, some betrayed their anxiety as they said good-bye to their loved ones. Several British nationals wrote farewell notes to their relatives in England and posted the letters on American soil. One passenger, Charles E. Lauriat, Jr., who was to survive the sinking, sought assurance that the *Lusitania* would be protected in the war zone. "When I bought my ticket at the Cunard office in Boston," he told a reporter, "I asked if we were to be convoyed through the war zone, and the reply was, 'Oh, yes! Every precaution will be taken.'" Similarly, when the Reverend Clark, another survivor, bought his ticket at the Cunard office in New York, he asked whether there was any extraordinary danger in traveling on the *Lusitania*. He was assured by the ticket agent: "No, none so far as I know. The Cunard Company is not likely to risk a ship of such enormous value if there were any extra danger."

The air was filled with rumors — all unsubstantiated. One had it that high Cunard officials had secretly warned their friends not to sail on the liner. After the disaster, Congressman Richard Pearson Hobson of Alabama charged: "A widowed cousin of mine applied at the New York office of the Cunard Line for passage on the *Lusitania*. The booking agent, an old friend, took her aside and told her that the vessel was acting under Admiralty orders and that she simply must not take passage on it. He pledged her to secrecy until after the trip."

This was a serious accusation against the Cunard Company. When it was brought to the attention of Charles P. Sumner, general manager of the company, he angrily dismissed the story as "absolutely false."

Another rumor had it that important passengers were being warned in person by German agents on the Cunard pier. Still another story was that certain passengers had received anonymous telegrams warning them not to leave on the liner. It was said that the young millionaire sportsman Alfred Gwynne Vanderbilt, son of Cornelius Vanderbilt, had received a message to this effect: "Have it on definite authority that the *Lusitania* is to be torpedoed. You had better cancel passage immediately." It was also said that Vanderbilt had received an added warning signed "*Morte*" (Death). Cunard agents who were on the ship charged that these and similar stories had been started by cranks.

Despite the warnings and the rumors, only a few persons canceled their passages at the last moment. Several transferred to the *New York*, an American Line ship operating weekly trips between England and New York. The American liner, which was a neutral vessel flying the United States flag, actually sailed a few hours later with unbooked space for more than 300 passengers, fully enough to have accommodated all the Americans who had left on the Cunarder. In Berlin, American Ambassador James W. Gerard had already supplied the German Foreign Office with full information on the sailings of the American Line as well as silhouettes of all its ships, including the *New York*.

At the pier, the Cunard Company took precautions to prevent any suspicious persons from boarding the *Lusitania* before she sailed. It required each passenger to get into line and personally claim his luggage. All packages, with the exception of trunks and valises, were to be opened. The voyagers passed in single file before a desk where their tickets were examined by Cunard clerks. Both officials and passengers acted as if these were merely standard operating procedures for a routine crossing.

The Queen of the Atlantic

THE "LUCY" was a magnificent ship, the current queen of the Cunard Line, and the fastest vessel on the seas. Lloyds of London had classed her as 100A-1. In 1915 terms, she was a floating castle.

The *Lusitania* and her sister ship the *Mauretania* were built of steel in 1907 by John Brown and Company, Limited, at Clydebank, Scotland, under British Admiralty survey and in accordance with Admiralty requirements. She was a four-stacker, fore and aft rigged, with eight decks, an overall length of 785 feet, a beam of 88 feet, and a depth of 60 feet 4½ inches. She had a total of 192 furnaces, six turbines of 68,000 indicated horsepower, and twenty-three double- and two single-ended boilers situated in four boiler rooms. When all boilers were working, the ship was capable of a speed of 24½ to 25 knots an hour. (A knot is equal to one nautical mile.)

Everything about the *Lusitania* was pitched to a gigantic scale. In her hull were 26,000 steel plates, several of which weighed as much as five tons each; these were held in place by 4,000,000 rivets. The rudder alone weighed 65 tons, and the three anchors weighed ten tons each. The main frames and beams, if placed end to end, would extend for 30 miles. Exactly 170 doors connected the various watertight compartments. There were 1,300 sidelights, 5,000 incandescent lights, and 200 miles of electrical wiring.

No expense had been spared to make this $10,000,000 liner the pride of the British passenger fleet. With competition intense between the major steamship lines, each company sought to make its great vessels the last words in luxury, but the *Lusitania*

THE CUNARD LINER "LUSITANIA;" LONGITUDINAL ELEVATION AND DECK PLANS.

CONSTRUCTED BY MESSRS. JOHN BROWN AND CO., LIMITED, SHIPBUILDERS AND ENGINEERS, CLYDEBANK.

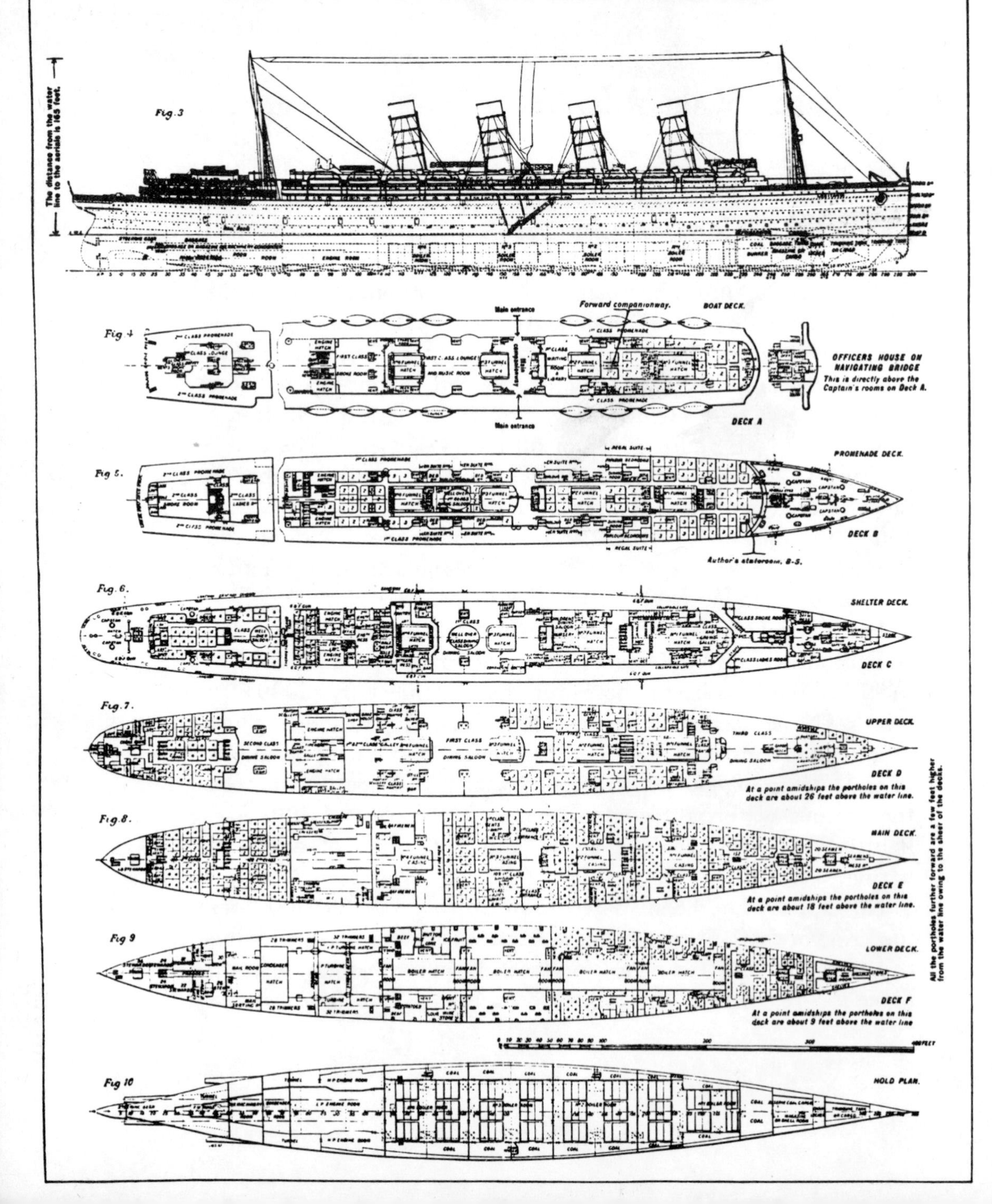

Longitudinal elevation and deck plans of the Cunard liner Lusitania.

dwarfed them all. Her cabins, lounges, theaters, restaurants — all fitted with expensive woodwork — were designed for a maximum of comfort and beauty. She was, as one proud Englishman said, a Goliath of the seas.

The *Lusitania* was launched in June, 1906, and made her maiden voyage in September, 1907. In 1908 she set a record by crossing the Atlantic from Queenstown to New York, a distance of 2,780 nautical miles, in 4 days and 15 hours.

The ship-makers of the Clyde, fine craftsmen, took special pains to ensure the floating capacity of the colossal ship; in fact, she was believed to be unsinkable. In most steamers of that time a series of walls divided the ship into cross sections so that if the hull were pierced the water would flood only one or two sections at most. To give her even more positive protection, however, the *Lusitania*'s designers had fitted her not only with these transverse bulkheads, dividing her into thirteen compartments, but also with two 425-foot longitudinal bulkheads, separating the side coal bunkers from the boiler rooms and engine rooms.

In the event of accident, any water entering the *Lusitania* was supposed to be confined not only to certain cross sections but also to a single side of these sections. This idea, originated by Navy designers and known as "battleship construction," was designed to increase the buoyancy of a ship in trouble. At the same time, however, the new device increased the sharpness of any list the ship might assume. And this was to have unfortunate consequences for the *Lusitania*.

Still another safety device was built into the huge Cunarder. Wherever it was necessary to have the doors of the bulkheads open for working the ship, these doors could be closed by hydraulic pressure from the bridge.

The *Lusitania* was not really unsinkable, but every safety factor then known to modern marine engineering had been used in her construction. This was in line with the Cunard Company's boast about its long safety record.

The builders of the *Lusitania* had also given painstaking attention to lifeboats and lifesaving apparatus. This was understandable in view of the sinking of the *Titanic*, the White Star liner which, on April 15, 1912, had hit an iceberg, with a loss of 1,513 persons out of 2,224 on board. Investigating commissions in both England and the United States had found that the *Titanic* did not have enough lifeboats and life belts. Everything possible had to be done to see that this tragedy was not repeated. Laws had been enacted calling for proper lifesaving facilities on all ocean liners.

There were forty-eight lifeboats on the *Lusitania*, of which twenty-two were ordinary Class-A lifeboats — eleven on each side of the boat deck. The remaining twenty-six were collapsible boats, eighteen of them stowed under the lifeboats, and eight placed on each side of the ship abaft the lifeboats. Each boat was provisioned with tanks of biscuits and water and was supposed to be in working order. The total capacity of the lifeboats and collapsible boats was about 2,607, substantially in excess of the requirements of the *Lusitania*'s last voyage.

To provide added safety, 2,325 life belts were distributed throughout the ship in racks and in staterooms. These were of two kinds: the familiar cork rings, and the new body belts. The latter were larger and clumsier than the cork rings, but supposedly more buoyant. About 125 belts were especially designed for children. Prominently displayed in each cabin was a notice giving the location of the life belts, and directions for putting them on. At strategic points on the decks there were thirty-two life buoys.

An emergency crew manned the *Lusitania* on her final voyage. Because the British navy was hard pressed for manpower when the war broke out in 1914, the Cunard Company had lost all its Royal Naval Reserve and Fleet Reserve employees, and had been forced to take on new men and train them hurriedly in positions of shipboard authority. It awarded prizes to the members of the crew who made themselves proficient in handling the lifeboats.

The *Lusitania* had accommodations for 2,198 passengers and a crew of about 850. Usually, about 2,000 people were carried on each voyage.

The Cunard Company felt that in the event of an emergency there would be plenty of room in the boats to take care of all the passengers and crew. There was a flaw in this reasoning: Suppose the boats on one side of the ship were rendered useless by a sudden and heavy list? This is precisely what happened to the *Lusitania* on her last trip.

May 1, 1915: The "Lusitania" Sails

AT 10:30 A.M. Saturday, May 1, 1915, the *Lusitania* backed from her pier on the North River and swung her nose downstream toward Sandy Hook and the open sea. The passengers lined the deck rails to get their customary last look at the New York skyline, the Statue of Liberty, Ellis Island, and Coney Island. They watched as a small boat came to pick up the pilot.

It was a fine spring day and the sea was smooth. Captain William Thomas Turner ordered the course steered on a circle toward Ireland.

The giant Cunarder carried 1,257 passengers on that fatal voyage — well below her capacity, but the largest number to be transported eastbound in a passenger vessel since the beginning of 1915. There were 702 members of the crew, making a total of 1,959 persons on board. There were 290 passengers in first class (saloon), 600 in second class (cabin), and 367 in third class (steerage). Of these, more than 900 were British and Canadian, and the remainder divided among eighteen other nationalities, including 6 Greeks, 3 Dutchmen, 1 Swiss, 5 Swedes, 3 Belgians, 2 Mexicans, 72 Russians, 8 Frenchmen, 2 Italians, 1 Indian, 1 Dane, 1 Spaniard, 1 Norwegian, 15 Persians, 1 Hindu, 1 Argentine, and 197 Americans.

The Lusitania *leaves New York, bound on her fatal voyage.*

United Press International Photo

Captain W. T. Turner, commander of the Lusitania *on her last voyage.*
United Press International Photo

Among the travelers were 688 adult males, 440 adult females, 51 male children, 39 female children, and 39 infants.

Captain Turner was an experienced officer who had held an Extra Master's Certificate since 1897. He had been in the service of the Cunard Company for thirty-two years, and since 1903 had held the position of commodore of the Cunard Line fleet. A former master of the *Aquitania* and other large Cunarders, he was making his second consecutive voyage on the *Lusitania.* There was also on board a second captain, J. C. Anderson, who was responsible for assisting in the care and navigation of the ship.

All the passengers knew that there was a war in Europe, and most knew of the German warning in *The New York Times,* but several who were traveling for business reasons felt that the chance to save a day or so by traveling on the fast liner was worth the danger. Others were attracted by the reduction in fares offered by the Cunard Company to attract more passengers at a time when many people were reluctant to cross the Atlantic. Some of the more lighthearted (and possibly light-headed) passengers seemed actually drawn by the possibility of danger. The State Department in Washington had been besieged with applications for passports and for special papers that would admit tourists to the zone of active operations to take combat photographs.

In addition to the world-famous Elbert Hubbard, millionaire Alfred Gwynne Vanderbilt, and popular playwright Charles Klein, there were other well-known Americans on board the *Lusitania.* Charles Frohman, the fifty-five-year-old "Napoleon of the Drama," had built up a famous theatrical empire. Another well-known passenger was the American novelist Justus Miles Forman.

The passengers quickly settled into the routine of transatlantic travel. They strolled on decks, read in deck chairs, played shuffleboard, drank at the bars, and played cards. The weather continued fair and the Atlantic was calm.

On the first evening out, as on succeeding nights, a pool for the following day's run was auctioned in the smoking rooms in an atmosphere of informality and ocean-liner camaraderie. The customary evening concert drew a large audience.

The next morning, Sunday, May 2, there was some fog. The first full run of twenty-four hours was announced as 501 nautical miles, an average of 21 miles per hour. This was well below the potential speed of the *Lusitania.* Several surprised passengers spoke to the officers about the slow pace, but were assured that all was in order.

What the passengers did not know was that on her last five round trips — including this, her final voyage — the *Lusitania* had run at an average speed of 21 knots, instead of her usual 24–25 knots. Even at this speed she was considerably faster than any transatlantic passenger liner at the time. The reduction in speed was partly for financial reasons — because of the lower-than-average passenger list — and partly to save coal and labor in time of war. Since November, 1914, the directors of the Cunard Company had run the *Lusitania* at three-fourths boiler power. Only nineteen of her twenty-five boilers were in use. Six of the boilers in No. 4 boiler space were not used at all.

From Monday to Friday the ship's run was well below the 500-mile mark. From Thursday noon to Friday noon it totaled just 484 miles.

There was gaiety aboard the liner, but it was outweighed by anxious discussions about the possibility of encountering a submarine. One passenger reported U-boats as the favorite subject of conversation. There would have been even more concern had the passengers known that more than a dozen Allied ships were sunk while the *Lusitania* was steaming toward her own rendezvous with disaster.

Captain Turner took the usual precautions as he approached the danger zone. He ordered the stewards to draw the shades in the salons and other public rooms as well as in the staterooms. He made certain that the lookouts were doubled, and placed two additional ones forward and one on either side of the bridge. There were two lookouts stationed in the crow's nest, two in the forecastle — the eyes of the ship; two officers were on the bridge at all times, and there was a quartermaster on each side of the ship. All were instructed to search for submarines. This was considered adequate visual coverage in the days preceding radar.

There was one bulkhead drill each day. In addition, a daily

The Lusitania *says farewell to her convoy on the high seas.*
United Press International Photo

boat drill for a picked crew was held each morning in a fixed emergency boat, either No. 13 on the starboard side, or No. 14 on the port side, according to the weather. A siren was blown, whereupon the special crew from the watch assembled at the boat, donned lifebelts, jumped into the boat, took their assigned places, and then jumped out again.

One of the passengers, Clinton Bernard, a New York mining engineer, later complained that he was not at all impressed by this drill:

I saw one so-called drill during the trip, which consisted of a boatswain blowing his whistle and a crew of six or seven men, many of whom had evidently never been to sea before, lining up on the deck. At a command from the boatswain the men jumped into a lifeboat, tied on life preservers and sat down. At another command they took off the preservers, stepped on the deck and were dismissed. The drill had been entirely satisfactory to the boatswain. It was impossible to see what benefit had been derived from it.

If Captain Turner had any doubts about the efficiency of his lifeboat crews, he said nothing about it at the time, nor did he order additional practice. Later he was to complain that his crew was not proficient in handling boats. "They are competent enough — they want practice. They do not practice enough, and they do not get the experience." The master was convinced that the old-time crews were better seamen.

One detail — apparently it was not enough to save lives — received careful attention. Each crew member had a boat badge with the number of the boat to which he was assigned.

Three days before the *Lusitania* was sunk, several of the more prominent passengers went to Captain Turner, told him that there was much talk among the passengers about submarines, and inquired if it were advisable to hold a boat drill for the passengers. It was essential, they said mildly, that the passengers know how to escape if the ship were torpedoed.

Captain Turner replied coolly that he was not worried about the danger and that he would get his ship to port safely.

"A torpedo can't get the *Lusitania*," he said, according to Francis Jenkins of New York. "She runs too fast."

The master dismissed his petitioners after assuring them that he would speak to the first officer about a drill for the passengers. It never took place. The passengers did, however, have the opportunity of consulting a boat list displayed at different places on the vessel.

Throughout Friday morning the ship went on with no sign of danger. By this time the lifeboats had been lowered to the promenade deck. The captain further ordered all bulkhead doors that were not necessary for the working of the ship to be closed.

Weather conditions were exceptionally good as the giant liner approached the Irish coast. There was a fog for a few hours, whereupon the ship's foghorn was blown until 10 A.M. But the fog, dismissed as morning mist, did not last long. The beautiful Irish littoral, resplendent in emerald green, was bathed in clear sunshine, and the sea was smooth as a mirror. The *Lusitania*, slowing down, was traveling about a dozen miles off the Irish coast at a rate of from 15 to 18 knots. Neither the captain nor any passenger was aware that three British torpedo boats lay at anchor in Queenstown (today called Cobh) all the time the Cunarder was coming up the Irish coast. The boats had been out in the morning, but they had come in so that the crews could have lunch.

At 11:30 A.M. the *Lusitania* received this message:

> *Submarines active in southern part of Irish Channel. Last heard of 20 miles south of Coningbeg Light Vessel. Make certain* Lusitania *gets this.*

At 1:00 P.M. the ship received a second message from the Admiralty:

Submarines 5 miles south of Cape Clear proceeding west when sighted at 10 A.M.

At this time Captain Turner altered his course inshore by about 30 degrees northward to either N. 63 or 67 E. mag. He thought he saw Galleyhead on the port bow, but he was not sure, and hence held inshore, maintaining his course for an hour.

Most of the ship's passengers were at lunch. A young Englishman, who had been served his ice cream, was waiting for the steward to bring him a spoon. He looked at his dessert and remarked humorously that he would hate to have a torpedo get him before he ate the ice cream.

Other diners laughed, a bit uncomfortably. One commented on how slowly the ship was running. It seemed that the engines had stopped.

In the meantime, several hours earlier on this fateful day, King George V had received Colonel Edward M. House, President Woodrow Wilson's emissary, in London.

"Suppose the Germans should sink the *Lusitania*?" the British monarch had asked Colonel House.

There is no record of a reply.

A Fateful Decision

AT THE END of Captain Turner's journey was Liverpool Bay, a danger area. The master of the *Lusitania* knew that several months earlier, on January 30, 1915, three British ships had been attacked by German U-boats in that vicinity. In addition, the *Camback* had been sunk by German submarines in Liverpool

Bay on February 20, and on March 9 the *Princess Victoria* had met a similar fate.

Before entering Liverpool Bay, the *Lusitania*'s master had to take his ship across Liverpool Bar, just 12 miles from Liverpool itself. The bar could be crossed only at high tide, which was due at 6:53 on the morning of May 8. This meant that Captain Turner would have to pass through Saint George's Channel in the darkness and cross the bar without stopping, at close to 4:00 A.M. The Cunard Company had given him permission to go ahead without a pilot.

It would have been difficult for Captain Turner to run close to Liverpool Bar on dead reckoning only. He would have to approach the Irish coast just long enough to make a formal landfall (a sighting or making land when at sea). From experience he knew that he must decide whether to keep offshore at approximately the same distance as he was when he passed Fastnet, or to work in to shore and go in close to Coningbeg Light Vessel. He weighed each possibility carefully, then decided on the latter course because he could then avoid any submarines reported lurking in mid-channel ahead of him. The trick was to delay this operation until exactly the right moment.

It was not an easy task. Not only did Captain Turner have the problem of navigating his ship safely to Liverpool, he would also have to maintain a sharp lookout for submarines. The British Admiralty, issuing general and specific orders, had repeatedly warned him of the menace; between midnight of May 6–7, and 10:00 A.M. on May 7, Captain Turner received the same warning seven times.

As the giant Cunarder approached the Irish coast at 8:00 A.M. on May 7, it encountered an intermittent fog — or Scotch mist — called "banks" by seamen. Captain Turner further reduced the speed of his ship from 18 to 15 knots. He was determined to run the last leg of his voyage before daylight the next morning.

Between 8:00 A.M. and 11:00 A.M. the *Lusitania* passed south of Fastnet Rock Lighthouse, which was not yet in sight but which was from 18½ to 25 miles distant. Captain Turner held up the course of his ship slightly to bring her closer to land. By noon the fog disappeared, and he increased the ship's speed to 18 knots. Just a little after noon, land was sighted abaft the port beam.

On that same Friday morning, May 7, young Captain Walther Schwieger, of the German submarine *U-20,* surfaced his boat about 12 miles off the Old Head of Kinsale, Ireland. He had left Emden a week ago in search of Allied ships, and was now preparing to return to base with his crew of thirty-five men and six officers. The last forty-eight hours had been successful ones: he had shelled a sailing ship and sunk two British steamers.

Suddenly Karl Scherb, one of the U-boat's officers, shouted that a large steamer was approaching ahead and to starboard. The ship, with four funnels and two masts, was coming in from south-southwest toward Galleyhead and was running on a course at right angles to that of the submarine.

Reacting automatically to Scherb's shout, Captain Schwieger called his crew to battle stations and submerged the *U-20* to a depth of 220 feet. Should he, in accordance with international law, give the passengers and crew a chance to take to the lifeboats before he attacked? He thought of the experience of Captain Weddigen, who had recently lost his submarine and his life when he gave way to the humanitarian urge to warn a prospective victim. Remembering what had happened to other German submarine skippers in similar circumstances, Captain Schwieger

Lieutenant Captain Schweiger, commander of the U-20.

decided not to surface his craft and expose it to the danger of being rammed. He ordered full speed ahead for the *U-20.*

At 1:40 P.M., just when he sighted the Old Head of Kinsale, Captain Turner was on the course S. 87 E. mag. This was just what the U-boat skipper wanted. Now it was possible for him to approach for a shot. He immediately ordered his ship forward at maximum speed in order to gain a position directly ahead of the *Lusitania.*

Later, in May, 1935, Scherb was to state in Berlin that he had no idea the victim was the *Lusitania.* He never thought so large a ship as the *Lusitania* would be on her regular course. Wouldn't she have been warned away from the danger area by British Admiralty reports?

At 1:50 P.M. Captain Turner ordered an officer on the bridge to take a four-point bearing on the Old Head of Kinsale, about 10 to 15 miles off, as a means of ascertaining the exact position of his ship so that he could steer a course up to Coningbeg. To get a bearing would take from twenty minutes to half an hour. The captain believed that he had escaped the submarines mentioned by the Admiralty in its last two wireless messages.

Meanwhile, the *U-20* was running at her maximum speed in order to gain a position directly ahead of the oncoming ship. The submarine's crewmen were at their posts, tensely awaiting the moment of attack. On command, they sent a torpedo directly toward the target.

Captain Schwieger entered the professional details in his log:

3:10 P.M. *(Middle European Time; 2:10* P.M. *Greenwich Time): Clean bow shot at a distance of 700 meters* [*approximately* ½ *mile*] *(G-torpedo, three meters* [10 *feet*] *depth adjustment); angle 90°, estimated speed 22 knots.*

Torpedo hits starboard side directly behind the bridge.

The "Lusitania" Is Hit

"SHE WAS CUTTING the water like a razor!" a passenger later testified.

Leaping swiftly through the surface of the smooth, slack sea, the torpedo belched from the *U-20* left a white wake as it headed for the starboard side of the *Lusitania.* The Cunarder was about 250 miles from Liverpool.

Many passengers had just finished lunch. Dispersed around the decks of the liner, they were admiring the lovely emerald green of the Irish coastline off the port beam. Some, anxious and frightened, joined in the lookout for a possible submarine attack. The day was so clear that several passengers and crewmen saw either the submarine or the torpedo — or both —and later gave the following accounts:

Ernest Cowper, a Toronto newspaperman: "I was chatting with a friend at the rail about two o'clock when suddenly I caught a glimpse of the conning tower of a submarine about a thousand yards distant. I immediately called my friend's attention to it. We both saw the track of a torpedo . . ."

Oliver P. Bernard, passenger: "I think I can say I was one of the few people who really saw a torpedo discharged at the *Lusitania.* Coming on deck from the dining salon, I was leaning against the starboard rail of the ship when I saw the periscope of a submarine about 200 yards away. Then I noticed a long white streak of foam. It gave me the impression of frothy, sizzling water. Almost immediately there was a terrific impact, followed by an explosion."

Dr. Carl E. Foss, passenger: "I was traveling second class, and on May 7, I was leaning against the rail on the port side of the ship, looking off towards the Irish coast. It was just at 1:30 that I noticed something low in the water about a mile away."

The torpedo used by the *U-20* held about 420 pounds of explosives. It was capable of effecting a rupture of the *Lusitania*'s outer hull 30 to 40 feet horizontally and 10 to 15 feet vertically. There was no time for those on board to learn the extent of the

German papers ran this picture of the Lusitania *as the first torpedo struck her. Superimposed on the upper left is a picture of von Tirpitz, Grand Admiral of the German fleet.*

United Press International Photo

damage. All that was known was that the projectile tore a great cavity in the hull of the giant ship.

At the moment of impact there was a heavy, muffled sound, not unlike that of an arrow entering the canvas and straw of a target, but magnified a thousand times. Smoke and steam came up the *Lusitania*'s superstructure. The crippled mammoth trembled for a moment under the force of the blow. Few misunderstood what it was — the officers on the bridge; the passengers at lunch, in their cabins, and in the smoking rooms; the crew in the stokeholds — all knew at once what had happened.

Within thirty seconds there was a second explosion farther back toward the center of the ship. Almost everyone on board thought that another torpedo had struck, but this time the noise was considerably louder. A shower of debris, coal, and water burst upward in a huge, dense column through the amidships superstructure. Along with it was a blinding cloud of steam. The force was sufficiently powerful to blow portions of the splintered hull high into the air above the Marconi wires 165 feet above the water.

The cause of that second explosion has never been ascertained. German sources insisted that it was due to the munitions on board. Dudley Field Malone, Collector of the Port of New York, wrote in *The Nation* (January 23, 1923): "Whether this second explosion was due to bursting boilers or to the ignition of other explosives is mere speculation."

A stoker gave one clue: two of the boilers, he said, had been jammed together by the force of the exploding torpedo and jackknifed upward, resulting in another explosion. This makes sense, but in all probability we shall never know what actually happened.

The main steam pipes or boilers had been carried away. The sea entered Nos. 1 and 2 boiler rooms, while some or all the coal bunkers on the starboard side of Nos. 1 and 2 boiler rooms were flooded.

Nothing was working. All the lights were out. The ship was listing heavily. The chief engineer turned to the senior second engineer Andrew Cockburn and asked: "What can we possibly do now?"

"Absolutely nothing," Cockburn replied.

There was heavy loss of life among the engineers — including the chief engineer and many stokers.

With the steam gone, and the engines out of control, it was impossible to stop or reverse the ship. The *Lusitania* kept her forward momentum.

Robert Leith, the wireless telegrapher, was in the aft dining room when the torpedo struck. He dashed to the Marconi house on the hurricane deck, where his assistant, David McCormick, was on duty. Orders came quickly from the bridge. This message was sent out and reiterated:

COME AT ONCE. BIG LIST TO STARBOARD.
TEN MILES OFF KINSALE.

At first the message was sent out by the ship's dynamo, but in three or four minutes this power gave out, and further calls were sent out by means of the emergency apparatus in the Marconi house. A wireless coastal station acknowledged the first signal almost immediately. The operators remained at their posts until a few moments before the ship went under. Leith was rescued, McCormick lost.

Unable to halt the forward momentum of the ship, Captain Turner judged it best not to launch the lifeboats until the vessel should lose her headway. He was confident that the *Lusitania* would stay afloat. He had faith in the ship's longitudinal bulkheads which, he believed — as did experienced architects — would give increased buoyancy to the ship. Actually, these bulkheads were inclined to give more sharpness to any list — and the *Lusitania* was beginning to list.

Captain Turner ordered Staff Captain Anderson, who was in charge of the port-side boats, to lower the lifeboats. Anderson, in turn, passed on this order to other officers.

List to Starboard

"THOSE ENGLISH PEOPLE are wonderful! So cool and so unexcited. You would think that nothing unusual had happened."

That was what Julian de Ayala, Consul General for Cuba at Liverpool, said later about the officers and crew on the sinking *Lusitania*. Others agreed that officers, stewards, and crewmen behaved exceedingly well under the tragic circumstances, but as always in moments of terrible stress there were differing reactions. Some passengers had the opposite point of view and accused the *Lusitania*'s officers of stupid overconfidence. According to Dr. J. T. Houghton of Troy, New York, just after the torpedo struck, an officer of the vessel had told him that there was no danger and that the ship would be headed for Queenstown and beached there. In the meantime, the officer had continued, the lifeboats would be made ready for an emergency.

This adverse view was also held by Dr. Howard Fisher, brother of Walter L. Fisher, United States Secretary of the Interior, who reported: "We then saw our first glimpse of an officer, who came along the deck and spoke to Lady Mackworth, Miss Conner, and myself, who were standing in a group. He said: 'Don't worry; the ship will right itself.' He had hardly moved on before the ship turned sideways, and then seemed to plunge headforemost into the sea."

Within minutes after the torpedo struck, there was a rush for the decks and for the lifeboats. Most witnesses later reported that there was no real panic, but there was confusion. Hundreds of people, fighting the increasing list to starboard (right) of the ship, crowded the staircases. The first-class passengers reached the decks quickly, and a majority of the second-class passengers got there, too, with the exception of several who had fainted in the dining room. Then the third-class passengers swarmed to the boats, and conditions became more chaotic.

Passengers and crewmen struggled to put on their life belts. Few of the travelers knew how to get into the new body belts.

Officers rescued from the Lusitania. *Reading from left to right are G. D. Lewis, Third Officer; A. A. Bester, Jr., Third Officer; A. R. Jones, First Officer.*
United Press International Photo

Some hung them around their waists, others wore them upside down. One man had his arm through one armhole and his head through the other. Some passengers and crewmen could be seen helping others to get into the clumsy things; but many, in the wild scramble for safety, thought only of themselves. Again and again officers and crewmen assured the terrified passengers that there was no danger — the ship was too close to shore.

Among the passengers there were a few who simply wandered around the decks or through the labyrinth of corridors, desperately trying to hold their balance. They were actually in a state of shock, too dazed and horrified to understand what had happened or what they were doing. Several were petrified into doing nothing at all.

Just before the torpedo struck, Elbert Hubbard and his wife were standing by the rail, a little forward of the entrance. Hubbard remarked jokingly that he did not believe he would be a welcome visitor in Germany because of a little essay he had written, entitled "Who Lifted the Lid Off Hell?" The torpedo struck, and the Hubbards remained in their position at the rail, he with his arm still around her waist. Charles E. Lauriat, Jr., a Bostonian, who had been standing nearby, suggested that they go to their stateroom — only a few minutes away — to get their life belts. The Hubbards did not move.

The main decks were becoming dangerously jammed with people as still more passengers crowded up from the steerage. A first-class passenger, Robert James Timmis, tried to reassure a group of panicked "Russians and other passengers" that the ship was safe; a steward had just told him so. "I could not talk to them," he said later, "but when I put up my hand and nodded my head and said, 'All right, all right,' they seemed to understand that. One of them kissed my hand, the first time I had ever had my hand kissed."

Meanwhile, both passengers and crew had begun to struggle with the collapsible boats, or life rafts, which were moored to the deck below the lifeboats. These boats were supposed to be lowered by the same davits that worked the open lifeboats above them, but there was so much trouble with the open lifeboats that there was little time to launch the life rafts. Fortunately, they were designed to float free if the ship should sink before they could be hoisted over the side.

Most passengers had no idea of how the collapsible boats worked. Men lost precious minutes trying to free the rafts from the deck or from the bars that held them and supported the lifeboat cradles. The ends of some rafts had been painted fast and were virtually glued to the deck. On some the hinges were rusty and the tackle was stiff from the dried paint and want of use. Several were caught together, one on top of the other, and could not be moved. All were so complicated that only a trained crew or a patient gadgeteer could have handled them.

Finally, with the strength of desperation, several passengers managed to wrench away a few of the life rafts. As the *Lusitania* went under, only minutes later, several more rafts floated free. One survivor counted six rafts afloat, two rigged and manned, and four overturned.

Robertson, the ship's carpenter, later claimed that the collapsible boats were piled, and the pins and gears in them examined, before the *Lusitania* sailed from New York. When the ship was struck, he said, he gave orders to the stewards standing around to clear away the collapsible boats, but the boats could not be launched in the confusion. The rafts were tied down so that they could not be scattered over the deck if the ship rolled.

"It would not have been proper to loose those collapsible boats in the war zone," Robertson said, "because you might do as much damage to the passengers by loosening the boats as otherwise. As the *Lusitania* was listing, if they had been unstrapped they would have encumbered the deck on the port side, but they would have fallen off the ship on the starboard side. These collapsible boats were never put amidships on the *Lusitania*, although they were on the *Aquitania*.

"I loosened all the collapsible boats on the port side and then went for my life belt. When I came up I noticed one of the boats, 21-E on the starboard side, still fast, and I loosened that. I was busy at that when I was washed into the sea, or slipped into the

This stoker, named Turner, survived not only the sinking of the Lusitania *but also those of* The Queen of Ireland *and the* Titanic. *He was known as "the man who could not be drowned."*

United Press International Photo

sea. That was the moment the ship disappeared. I saw three of the collapsible boats, one on top of the other. With some other crewmen I got them separated. We picked up about twenty-seven people."

Many passengers, some hysterically and some calmly, decided that it was useless to try to launch the lifeboats, and leaped overboard. Bodies hit the water with fearful crashes. Some passengers waited until the water was flush with the main deck, and then slipped quietly into the sea. Others let themselves down with ropes. Hundreds, trapped aboard, went down with the ship.

Most desperate of all was the plight of the 129 children who could not help themselves. Passengers and crewmen stripped off their own life belts and fastened them around the children, but in most cases it was a useless gesture. Only 35 little ones were saved. Mothers went under the water with their children in their arms. The bodies of boys and girls who had died from drowning, shock, or exposure, were later seen floating on the water.

Disaster on the Port Side

MEANWHILE, there was bad trouble on the port (left) side of the ship. Here were lodged the even-numbered lifeboats, 2 to 22, for which Staff Captain Anderson, who was on the bridge when the torpedo struck, was responsible. In charge of boats 2 to 10 was Albert Arthur Bestwick, the junior third officer. Should an emergency develop, he was to be assisted by the second officer.

As the *Lusitania* listed to starboard, the lifeboats on the port side swung inward. This made it not only difficult but almost impossible to lower those on the port side. "To lower the port boats," the ship's carpenter later testified, "would be just like drawing a crate of unpacked china along a dock road. What I mean is that if you started to lower the boats you would be dragging them down the rough side of the ship on rivets which are what we call 'snaphead' rivets. They stand up about an inch from the shell of the ship, so that you would be dragging the whole side of the ship away if you tried to lower the boats with a 15-degree list."

Nevertheless, heroic efforts were made to get these port boats away in the eighteen minutes the *Lusitania* stayed afloat. The boat swinging just opposite from the grand entrance on the port

Newly arrived survivors in Queenstown.
United Press International

side was smashed against the side of the ship, throwing all its occupants into the sea.

How many of the port lifeboats got away remains a mystery. Bestwick was certain that numbers 2, 4, 6, 8, and 10 were not launched. This is understandable in view of the fact that these boats were on the forward end of the port side and the *Lusitania* was going down bow-first. Two of these lifeboats are said to have been successfully launched, but one filled with water within five minutes and had to be abandoned, while the second never reached Queenstown.

Isaac Lehman, a New York export broker, wrote the following story for *The New York Times:**

As usual, I had luncheon at one o'clock in the main dining room, situated on D Deck. After luncheon was through — about 1:30 — I went upstairs on A Deck to the smoking room and sat by the window on the English side of the land. We had passed the Irish coast some hours before and were just coming into sight of the English side.

I wrote some letters home, and had just finished writing these letters and some postal cards. . . . All of a sudden we heard a noise like the boom of a cannon, and I said to Medbury: "They have got us at last!" He thought I was joking. My answer was, "Let's go outside and see if I am joking."

I rushed through the smoking room to the deck and turned and saw the torpedo making direct for us. The time from the noise of the report until it struck us was less than a minute. I said, "Let's get away from here; it looks as if it is going to strike right under us." I do not know what became of Mr. Medbury after that.

I went to the other side of the deck to the last lifeboat before the second class came along. Everybody by this time was on deck and the boat was shaking like a leaf from the effect of its being hit by the torpedo. When I reached the first lifeboat nobody had made an effort to get it ready for lowering, and I suggested to the different gentlemen around there to get it ready.

A great many people got into the lifeboat and there were three or four men at each rope to lower the boat, one man standing there with a hatchet in his hand to cut the blocks. One side started lowering the boat and the other did not, and as a result, before anybody knew what had happened, the other fellows let go and the rope broke which *held the lifeboat and threw everybody into the sea, the boat finally breaking from the davits itself and dropping into the water.*

After I had seen this I rushed down the deck to the entrance which is known as the grand entrance and ran down to the D Deck to my stateroom, known as D-48, to get a life preserver. I don't know whatever possessed me, but I looked in my dress suitcase and got hold of my revolver, as I figured this would come in handy in case there was anybody not doing the proper thing.

I walked up to B Deck and met my steward — by the name of Barnes — on the way, and I told him to get me a life preserver. I waited for him to get this, and he put it on for me, saying that it would come in handy. I walked out on B Deck and met the ship's doctor and the ship's purser, who told me there was not a chance for the boat to go down, that I should remain calm, and said I was foolish to have my life preserver on.

I rushed up to A Deck. I reached the second lifeboat and stood on one of the collapsible boats, which lay on the deck covered with canvas. There were quite thirty or forty people in the boat already, and I asked why this boat was not launched and put down into the sea. I turned and looked to the front part of the ship, and she was so far settled down in the water that there was no chance that the Lusitania *would not sink.*

I again asked why the boat was not put in the water, and said, "Who has got charge of this boat?" One man, who had an ax in his hand, answered that orders had been issued by the captain not to launch any boat. My reply was, "To hell with the captain! Don't you see the boat is sinking? And the first man that disobeys my orders to launch the boat I shoot to kill!"

I drew my revolver, and the order was then obeyed. The boat was just about started on its way down when the ship gave an awful lurch, as if foundering, and receded. There were thirty to forty men and women standing on the collapsible boat where I was, and the boat in receding smashed all these people, who were trying to get into the boat, up against the smoking room, killing pretty much all of them or injuring them so badly that they could not move, I being knocked down as well, and hurting my leg severely, but I succeeded in crawling out and was able to hold onto the rails when the water from the funnels commenced pouring over us.

A terrific explosion occurred in front of the steamer, and then I noticed that the lifeboat which had killed these people had gone back into its original position. By this time the ship was sinking fast, and this boat finally got away safely. I was then thrown high into the water, free and clear of all wreckage, and I then went down twice with the suction of the steamer, and the second time I came up I was 400 or 500 feet away from the ship. I clung to an oar, and just then I saw the Lusitania *take her final plunge. It sounded like a terrible moan.*

Immediately after she sank there were hundreds of people struggling in the water, praying and crying for help. There was wreckage all around — old chairs, wood, all kinds of smaller items — but taken all in all there was very little large wreckage. The water was not so cold and it was a lovely day, the sun shining and not a ripple on the water. Had the sea been the least bit rough, I do not believe that out of the entire lot that were living at the time she went down fifty would have been saved, as most of the boats that did get away had no plugs in them, and the collapsible boats that were floating had no oars in them.

The sights in the water around me defy description. Right near me were several men who watched with me for help. We saw, about a mile distant from the wreck, what we thought was a sailboat, which kept our hopes up, but we soon found out that this must have been the periscope of the submarine which sunk us, watching us.

Toward five o'clock torpedo boats and other boats came to our aid. I managed to keep alive by using my arms and my leg to keep warm, as toward sundown the water commenced to get very cold and I became very numb. I was only picked up — by Chief Officer Jones — about 6:15 in the evening, having been in the water from 2:28, as my watch stopped at that time, for almost four hours.

The Struggle for Life

THE *Lusitania*'s forward momentum had carried her from two to three miles from where she had been hit. By 2:20, a matter of minutes, she was settling along her entire waterline, her compartments hopelessly flooded. Slowly the stern of her great hulk rose into the air as she took an angle of 90 degrees and began to go down by the bow.

Roars of explosions thundered across the sea as cold water struck the boilers. It was an unearthly sound. The ship's huge machinery was cutting through the bulkheads as if they were butter. Frantic passengers, clustered on the port side, began to slide down toward the starboard side, dashing themselves against each other until they were engulfed by the water. Unlaunched lifeboats swung crazily from their davits. Collapsible boats slithered into the sea. Many people already in the lifeboats were thrown screaming into the water.

As the great ship made her final plunge — just eighteen minutes after the torpedo struck — she seemed to shorten; then, just as a duck dives, she went under. None of the funnels crashed. The *Lusitania* seemed to divide the water as smoothly as if she were a great knife cutting the sea. With her sank hundreds of trapped passengers and crewmen, her entire cargo, and the first American sacks of mail ever lost at sea as a result of war.

There remained on the spot a nondescript mass of floating wreckage — deck chairs, broken planking, crates, cylindrical drums, life belts. Hundreds of struggling swimmers thrashed around in the water, clinging to the wreckage and to each other. It was like some macabre pageant: a sea of waving arms and hands, as men, women, and children made desperate efforts to remain afloat in the maelstrom of debris and swirling water. There were agonizing cries of "My God!" "Help us!" "Please save us!" Women with children in their arms begged those in the boats to take their babies.

Gradually, the shouts and cries grew weaker on all sides. "Finally," said survivor Dr. Daniel V. More, an American physician, "there was a low weeping, wailing, inarticulate sound, mingled with coughing and gargling. It made me sick." It was the familiar sound of all such sea tragedies, described earlier by a British schoolmaster when the *Titanic* sank. "Then there fell on our ears the most appalling sound that human beings ever heard

A clergyman tries to comfort a dazed survivor.
United Press International

— the cries of hundreds of our fellow beings struggling in the icy water, crying for help with a cry that we knew could not be answered."

There was little suction or vortex as the *Lusitania* disappeared below the sea. It was probable, as Captain Turner later said, that the bow of the ship was already resting on the bottom when the stern went under. She sank in about 60 fathoms (360 feet) of water, and she was 785 feet long.

There were conflicting reports as to whether the propellers had stopped as the stern of the ship rose into the air. Some survivors said that the four giant screws were still turning; others were just as certain they had stopped, thereby lessening the suction at the spot of sinking. Instead of a sucking in, there was a curious shooting out from the stricken mammoth after she sank. This was caused in part by the inrush of water into her funnels with resulting explosions as the cold water encountered the steam of the boilers.

Captain Schwieger of the *U-20* was looking at the results of his work. Here are his reactions as he noted them in his diary:

> *3:10* [*2:10*] *An unusually heavy detonation follows with a very strong explosion cloud. (High in air over first smokestack.) Added to the explosion of the torpedo, there must have been a second explosion. (Boiler or coal or powder.) The superstructure over point struck and the high bridge are rent asunder; fire breaks out and smoke envelops the high bridge.*
>
> *The ship stops immediately and quickly heels to starboard, at the same time diving deeper by the bow. She has the appearance of being about to capsize. Great confusion on board, boats being cleared and part being lowered to water. They must have lost many heads. Many boats crowded came down bow first or stern first in the water and immediately fill and sink. Fewer lifeboats can be made clear on the port side owing to the slant of the boat.*
>
> *The ship blows off, in front appears the name* Lusitania *in gold letters. The stacks were painted black, no stern flag was up. She was running at a speed of 20 sea miles.*
>
> *3:25 It seems as if the vessel will be afloat only a short*

time. Submerge to 24 meters and go to sea. I could not have fired a second torpedo into this throng of humanity attempting to save themselves.

4:15 Go to 11 meters and take look around. In the distance astern are drifting a number of lifeboats. Of the Lusitania *nothing is to be seen. The wreck must lie off Old Head of Kinsale Lighthouse, in 358° N.W., 14 sea miles off in 90 meters of water (27 miles from Queenstown), 51°22.6′ N. and 8.32′ W. The shore and lighthouse are clearly seen.*

Captain Schwieger was satisfied with his work. Final entries in his diary noted that it was a mystery as to why the *Lusitania* was not sent through the North Channel, and that there was a surprising amount of traffic south of Saint George's Channel. He strongly recommended the area south of Ireland, from Fastnet Rock to Saint George's Channel, about 30 to 50 sea miles off the coast, as "one of the best areas for war on merchant ships." Steamers, he observed with professional acumen, could not possibly run through the night in this zone, if they also wanted to proceed by night through the Irish Sea.

At 4:08 P.M., when the rescue fleet from Queenstown was nearing the scene, Captain Schwieger sighted and attacked another Cunard ship, this time a freighter of about 7,000 tons, "with one thick red smokestack, two masts, without stern flag." Something was wrong with the torpedo — it got away, but missed the target.

The *U-20* submerged and headed home. Captain Schwieger had only one torpedo left in the stern tube of his submarine.

Chaos at Queenstown

AT ONE O'CLOCK on the afternoon of May 7, the *Swanmore* of the Johnson Line, running between Liverpool and Baltimore, Maryland, was just south of Daunt's Rock when she received an urgent wireless from the British Admiralty urging her to make haste for port. Captain Cowan ordered the speed of his ship increased from her usual 12 knots to 16 knots, with double shifts of passers and stokers called to duty.

The *Swanmore*, ironically, was just 30 miles from the *Lusitania* when the latter was torpedoed. Captain Cowan received her repeated calls for help, but he did not go to her aid, reasoning that it was his duty to follow Admiralty orders and bring his ship to port as quickly as possible. Here he was told that everybody on board the *Lusitania* had been lost.

The *Lusitania*'s SOS was received at Queenstown precisely at 2:15 P.M. Admiral Coke at once dispatched "all possible assistance" to the scene. But this "all possible assistance" did not include a flotilla of high-speed destroyers stationed at Queenstown. The Admiralty had forbidden all British naval vessels to go to the aid of torpedoed ships because they, in turn, might be sunk. It had not been forgotten that the armored cruisers *Cressy, Aboukir,* and *Hogue* had been torpedoed in quick succession on September 22, 1914, by Captain Weddigen of the *U-9*.

Although the *Lusitania* was about a dozen miles off the Irish coast when she was torpedoed, only a single trawler was in sight at the time. This small vessel did not arrive in time to save any of the swimmers, but it did gather in some 110 persons who were in lifeboats and life rafts.

From Queenstown, just 25 miles away, a motley fleet of rescue craft hastily put out to sea. Included among them were two torpedo boats, several sailboats, and the local Queenstown lifeboat towed by a tug. In addition, the *Flying Fox*, a tender that customarily went out from Queenstown to meet incoming steamers, saved 80 people. Among the half-dozen trawlers was the *Indian Empire*, which picked up from 70 to 80 survivors. The motorboat *Elizabeth* gathered 60 persons from one lifeboat and 16 from another. A Manx fishing smack took on a load of passengers, while another, the *Bluebell*, rescued — among others — Captain Turner. Additional survivors boarded the tugs *Warrior*, *Julia*, and *Stormcock*, this last rescuing more than 150 survivors.

There was little organization in this fleet of small boats; but there was will, courage, and pity. Like the famous amateur fleet at Dunkirk in World War II, the rescuers were interested only in getting there as quickly as they could and in saving as many lives as possible.

The largest rescue ship — and a godsend for the survivors — was a tramp steamer, the *Katarina*, which flew the Greek flag. She took on board the occupants of several lifeboats and later transferred them to the rescue fleet. The survivors found neither clothing nor beds on the Greek ship, but they were at least safe. And aboard the *Katarina* was an Italian surgeon who went to work to help the victims. The arm of one of his patients was hanging by the skin, whereupon he amputated the arm with a butcher's knife.

The fleet of rescue craft began to reach the lifeboats and flotsam between 5:00 and 6:00 P.M. It was a heartrending scene. Strewn over the sea was all that remained of the mammoth greyhound, her passengers, her crew. Floating in all directions was a jumble of lifeboats, rafts, and the accumulated paraphernalia of sea disaster.

John Roper (right), crewman, who rescued Captain Turner and later went back to rescue seventeen other survivors from the sea.

United Press International Photo

Several lifeboats were rowed by survivors to fishing smacks a few miles off Kinsale before the rescue fleet arrived. These people were then transferred to the small boats coming from Queenstown. On occasion, the rescued called: "We're all right! Go to the others!"

The rescuers did what they could for the rescued. Although not equipped with relief devices, most of the craft were able to supply shelter and warm drinks to the survivors. Skippers and crew members stripped their own garments and gave them to the victims.

Passengers and redheaded cockney crew members manned one of the collapsible boats converted into a lifeboat. The make-

Members of the Lusitania's *crew.*
United Press International Photo

shift crew started to row for shore and steered for the Old Head of Kinsale. Off in the distance they saw a lone man floating by himself. He seemed to prefer his own company, until suddenly he saw the boat and began yelling for help. He was picked up. After rowing for nearly three miles, the crew came to a small fishing smack, which had already taken on board two boatloads but which graciously made room for the newcomers.

The elderly fishermen could not do enough for their new passengers. They started a fire, boiled water, made tea. There were no cabins on the smack, hence all hands had to remain on the deck, which was so covered with fish scales that it was difficult to stand upright. Some survivors removed their clothing, only to become thoroughly chilled. After remaining on the fishing smack until 6:00 P.M., they were transferred to the tender, *Flying Fox.* The sea was so calm that the people merely had to step across the space from the fishing boat to the old packet.

For nearly three hours the rescue craft beat back and forth over the sea where the *Lusitania* had gone down. By this time the lifeboats, rafts, and wreckage were dispersed over a large area.

Corpses were piled on the rescue ships as they reached Queenstown. On one of the rescue flotilla, a handsome young woman was quickly dragged out of a pile of corpses when someone noticed her eyelids flutter. She seemed to be none the worse for her experiences. At the Queenstown wharves drowned victims

These two women were rescued after many hours in the water.
United Press International Photo

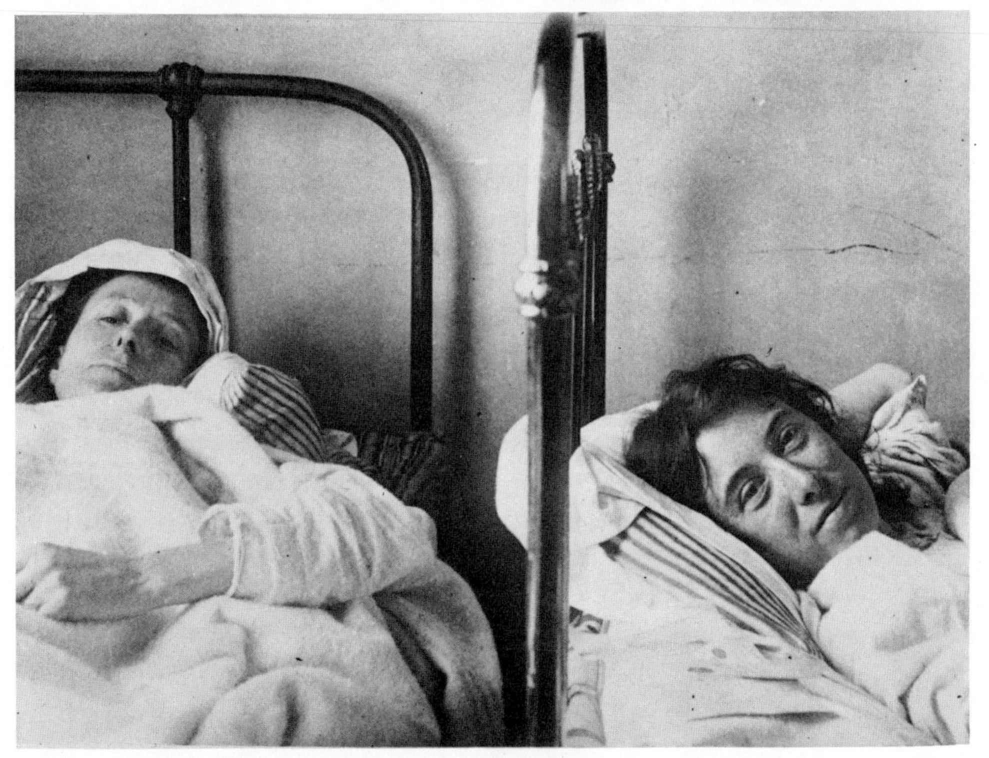

were piled in even rows among the coils of rope and paint barrels. It was a weird, ghastly spectacle — the glaring gas torches throwing flickering shadows over the bodies piled like cordwood.

Three improvised morgues were set up for the dead: one at Town Hall, one at the Cunard dock, and a third at a disused ship chandlery on Harbour Row. There was no refrigeration available for the bodies — artificial preservation was considered unnecessary because of the climate.

In the dimly lit morgues, silent policemen walked slowly up and down the aisles making up lists describing the bodies. Sobbing relatives passed between the rows of corpses searching for their loved ones. It was a pitiful sight: young children on the slabs; a half-dozen dead mothers with babies clasped in their arms; one mother with a dead infant at each breast. Among the bodies were several beautiful young American girls.

All available caskets at Cork and Queenstown were instantly used up. It was decided not to await further caskets from London. Leaden cases were quickly constructed at Cork and transferred to Queenstown.

On Monday afternoon a mass funeral, attended by sympathetic Irishmen and military, naval, and civilian officials, was held along the hillside about a mile from Queenstown. Volunteer squads of British soldiers dug four collective graves. Some 140 unknown bodies were buried in these great pits, but eventually only 65 remained unidentified. Various religious services were held for the dead.

That same afternoon a search began for more survivors, floating bodies, and corpses washed up on the coast. A half-dozen specially chartered tugs searched repeatedly for over a month along 250 miles of the Irish coastline for bodies that had been scattered by the Gulf Stream and by strong easterly winds com-

Mass graves on the coast of Ireland, where the bodies of those who were washed up by the sea were buried.

United Press International Photo

ing directly from England. One body was recovered in County Galway more than 200 miles from the scene of the sinking. More than 900 corpses were never recovered.

The body of Alfred Gwynne Vanderbilt was never found. Representatives of the Vanderbilt estate came to Queenstown and for two weeks directed a search along the southwest coast for the young American millionaire. A reward of £400 was offered for recovery of the body — a fantastic sum, at the time, to the poor Kerry fishermen. The reward was never claimed.

Bodies continued to appear in June and July after the searching operations had been discontinued. The corpses had remained

Survivors of the Lusitania *wait at Queenstown station for a train to London.*
United Press International Photo

below the surface of the sea and floated only after decomposition had set in. This word picture of the recovered corpses was given by the American Consul Frost: "The rigidity of the bodies had relaxed into inebriate flabbiness, features were broken down into preposterously animal-like repulsiveness. Faces registered every shading of the grotesque and hideous. Lips and noses were eaten away by seabirds, and eyes gouged out into staring pools of blood. Toward the last the flesh had gone from grinning skulls, the trunks were bloated and distended with gases, and limbs were partially eaten away or bitten clean off by sea creatures so that stumps of raw bones were left projecting."

Impact: The Battle of Words

THE NEWS hit London with the impact of a hurricane.

At first people refused to believe it. On the Strand a newsboy shouted, "*Lusitania* torpedoed and sunk! Official!" He was stopped outside the Hotel Cecil by a police constable who told the lad that he would be arrested if he were crying out false news. The boy at once showed the curious policeman the official report of the disaster in the "Stop-Press Column." He was allowed to proceed. In a few minutes he was surrounded by a clamoring crowd which bought all his newspapers.

The sinking was the sole topic of conversation all over London. For once the English reputation for understatement failed. One after another, in bitter tones, they denounced the Germans. The offices of the Cunard Company were besieged with relatives begging for news of the disaster.

Anti-German feeling coursed not only in London but throughout all England. In Liverpool a crowd gathered in front of a German cutlery shop and began heaving bricks through the window. In a few minutes the place was a wreck. An eyewitness described it: "Then everyone broke into the place and soon all the furniture, carpets, and everything else was thrown out of the windows into the street. There were several policemen at the corner, half a block away, and they only grinned. The crowd then went on down the street and wrecked four German pork shops and carried away some of the meat. I saw one young fellow going off with half a hog, and an old woman was dancing in the middle of the streets with strings of sausages all over her and flying in the wind, while the crowd cheered."

This was notably un-British behavior, but it was typical of

The Cunard Company's office, jammed with people waiting for news of those who had sailed on the Lusitania.

United Press International Photo

demonstrations by an angered populace. The London Royal Exchange and some provincial exchanges decided to exclude persons of German birth. On May 11, just a few days after the sinking, a procession of businessmen marched from the city to the House of Commons to press the government to take further repressive steps against Germans living in England. There was quick action. Two days later, on May 13, it was announced that, in addition to the 19,000 enemy aliens already registered in England, all males of German, Austro-Hungarian, or Turkish origin who were within the military age bracket of seventeen to forty-five and who had not been naturalized would be segregated and interned.

The London *Times* was appalled by the sinking: "The full horror of the *Lusitania* has now been revealed. . . . Unless Berlin is entered, all the blood which has been shed will have flowed in vain." Prominent Britons denounced the sinking as cold-blooded mass murder of helpless men, women, and children, and as a shocking violation of the rights of humanity. Lord Wearsdale, president of the Anglo-American Centennial Committee, was bitter: "Language is inadequate to condemn the atrocious criminals who have deliberately adopted piracy and the murder of innocent civilians as the methods of warfare. The conscience of Christian Germany will protest against it."

Responsible Britons predicted that there would be a strong American reaction to the deed. Lord Sydenham of Combe, former governor of Bombay, announced that "Americans will now realize the depths of German barbarism, and respond to the call of humanity." Novelist Sir Gilbert Parker excoriated the Germans for an "infamous crime" and added: "It is an international business, and not England alone will take note of it. The United States will have something to say in regard to the destruction of life and property, which, in one sense, is as much her's as Britain's."

Many Englishmen hoped that the tragedy would bring the United States into the war against a common enemy. Admiral Cyphrian Bridge was hopeful: "At first sight this outrageous crime, outdoing the acts of the cruelest pirates ever known, seems to have been deliberately perpetrated, with the intention of defying and exasperating the American people. Considering the warning given Germany by the United States government, it is hardly conceivable that the United States will abstain from punishing the crime and preventing the repetition by forcible means."

Within a few hours after the sinking of the *Lusitania*, the American ambassador to Great Britain, Walter Hines Page,

Unidentified mother and boy rescued from the Lusitania.

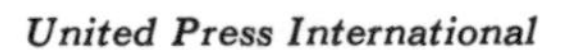

United Press International

Two survivors of the Lusitania *as they land at Queenstown.*

United Press International Photo

Kathleen Kaye, who helped row the lifeboat in which she was saved, and H. G. Colebrook, who still carries the life belt that kept him afloat.

United Press International

The boy in bed is Frank Hook, who jumped from the second deck of the Lusitania, *only to have a boat fall on him and break his arm.*

United Press International Photo

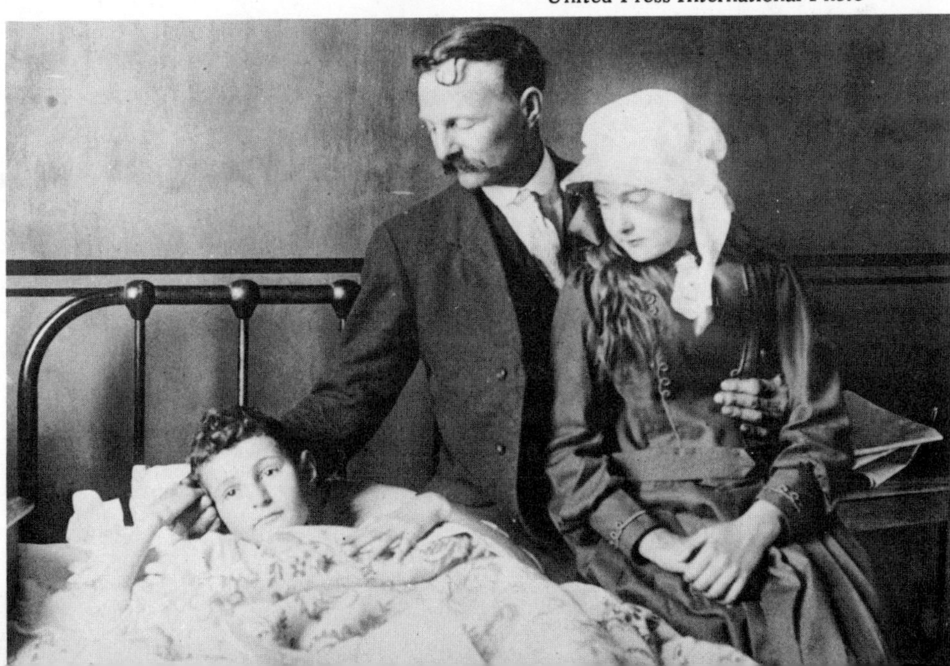

called for immediate intervention. Page cabled Wilson: "The United States must declare war or forfeit European respect."

When Colonel Edward M. House, friend and adviser of President Woodrow Wilson, was told of the sinking, he foresaw a declaration of war within a month. House, who was in London, cabled the President: "America has come to the parting of the ways, when she must determine whether she stands for civilized or uncivilized warfare. We can no longer remain neutral spectators."

Other prominent Americans in Europe were equally angered. In Berlin, James W. Gerard, the American ambassador, prepared to leave his post, as did Brand Whitlock in Belgium. Herbert Hoover, then in charge of Belgian relief, began to ship all the food he could get into Belgium, on the assumption that America would immediately break her relations with Germany.

In the United States there was a similar reaction of disbelief, bewilderment, denunciation. There was one exception — in New York, German-Americans drank to "the great victory of the *Vaterland*" in Yorkville casinos and restaurants.

The New York Times, under its brilliant managing editor, Carr Vattell Van Anda, put out a predawn extra on May 8, 1915, that surpassed anything of its kind. It was one of the great journalistic triumphs of the twentieth century.

Van Anda's headlines over the story were as follows:

LUSITANIA SUNK BY A SUBMARINE, PROBABLY 1,260 DEAD; TWICE TORPEDOED OFF IRISH COAST; SINKS IN 15 MINUTES; CAPT. TURNER SAVED, FROHMAN AND VANDERBILT MISSING; WASHINGTON BELIEVES THAT A GRAVE CRISIS IS AT HAND

The fourth line was based on a story out of Washington that said: "Although they are profoundly reticent, officials realize that the tragedy, involving the lives of American citizens, is likely to bring about a crisis in the international relations of the United States."

Van Anda devoted the whole of his front page, as well as several inside pages, to the story. His handling was objective, in contrast to the emotionalism of other editors. His front page contained the news story; a picture of the *Lusitania*; an eyewitness report dated Queenstown, Saturday, May 8, 3:18 A.M., by Ernest Cowper, a Toronto newspaperman; a list of the rescued; a story of the anxious crowds at the New York Cunard office; and reactions from Washington and London. The inside pages included extraordinarily fast coverage with pictured cross sections of the *Lusitania*; photographs and biographies of the prominent passengers and Captain Turner; sailing lists; eyewitness reports; and comment from the foreign press. The staff of the *Times* worked feverishly through the night to produce what turned out to be the famous 8:30 A.M. EXTRA edition.

The New York *World* expressed its indignation over the *Lusitania*'s sinking in these words:

> *It is no fault of the German government that every American on board the* Lusitania *is not lying on the bottom of the sea. The whole German submarine policy, in its campaign not against British ships of war, but against merchantmen on the high seas, is a revival of piracy — piracy organized, systematized, and nationalized.*

The contention that Germany must have gone berserk was echoed throughout the American press. The Richmond (Virginia) *Times-Dispatch* said:

Germany must surely have gone mad. The torpedoing and sinking of the Lusitania *evince a reckless disregard of the opinions of the world in general and of this country in particular.*

Another Richmond newspaper, the *Evening Journal*, said:

This act is wholesale, cowardly, deliberate assassination. No massacre ever done by savage people, by Indians and wild Africans, was so base, cruel, and ruthless. The savages at least attacked in the open and encountered some risk.

The Louisville (Kentucky) *Courier-Journal* excoriated both Germany and the Kaiser:

Truly, the nation of the Black Hand and the bloody heart has got in its work. Nothing in the annals of piracy can, in wanton and cruel ferocity, equal the destruction of the Lusitania.

Exultation in Germany

INSIDE GERMANY the news of the sinking of the *Lusitania* was hailed with satisfaction. Hundreds of congratulatory telegrams were sent to Admiral Alfred von Tirpitz. In Magdeburg the enthusiasm was so great that a local committee was formed to collect money to be used as a national gift for the officers and crew of the *U-20*. There was praise for "the pluck and daring" of those men. Buildings were decorated with flags. Schoolchildren were given a half-holiday.

The Fatherland (Das Vaterland), a journal, published "The Hymn of the *Lusitania*" by an unnamed poet:

> *Yes, ten such ships are a paltry fine*
> *For one good life in our fighting line.*
> *Let England ponder the crimson text —*
> *"Torpedo, strike, and hurrah for the next!"*

Mixed with the exultation was a deep sense of guilt. Germans competed with one another to justify the sinking. Typical was the comment of Baron Mumm von Schwartzenstein, an important diplomat in the German Foreign Office: "Nobody regrets more sincerely than we Germans the hard necessity of sending to their deaths hundreds of men. Yet . . . the scene of war is no golf links, the ships of belligerent powers no pleasure places. The sinking of the *Lusitania* was for us a military necessity."

Behind the reaction was a tremendous yearning for victory. The Germans had gone to war on August 4, 1914, with an outburst of popular enthusiasm. This was not unique — there had been equally extravagant scenes in Paris, London, and St. Petersburg — but the Germans were convinced that destiny owed them victory and a "place in the sun." This was supposed to be a short and beautiful war, but it had not worked out that way. Disillusionment set in as the war reached a stalemate and the casualty lists mounted. The German advance had been halted at the Marne, and the Imperial armies driven back to the Aisne River. The Allies had been victorious in the race to the sea and they held Calais, Boulogne, and Dunkirk, thereby ensuring communication between England and France. By the end of 1915, the Allies were almost complete masters of the seas. The German plan for a quick and decisive victory had miscarried.

And now came this news of a German "triumph" — the sinking of the *Lusitania.*

The *Kolnische Volkszeitung* received the news happily: "With joyful pride we contemplate this latest deed of our navy."

The *Deutsche Tageszeitung* attacked the British: "The passengers who went down with the *Lusitania* are, if we wish to call things by their right name, a sacrifice to Great Britain's frivolity and avarice."

The Berlin *Lokalanzeiger* was harsh: "We do not want any love from the Americans, but we do want respect, and the case of the *Lusitania* will win it for us better than a hundred victims on land."

"We rejoice over this new success of the German navy," said the *Neue Freie Presse.*

The famous *Lusitania* medal appeared soon after the sinking. Designed by the artist Karl Goetz, the medal showed on the obverse (front) side a skeletal figure of Death at the Cunard office selling tickets. A passenger carried a newspaper with the words "SUBMARINE DANGER," while a German held up a warning finger. The major inscription was "BUSINESS FIRST."

The reverse side showed the *Lusitania* — with a ram like a battleship, and laden with munitions, airplanes, and contraband — sinking. The legend above read "NO CONTRABAND," and below: "The liner *Lusitania* sunk by a German submarine, 5 May 1915."

Note that the day of the sinking was given as *May 5* instead of May 7. For Allied propagandists this was a heaven-sent opportunity. They charged that this was proof beyond a shadow of a doubt that Germany had planned the sinking and had struck off the medal even before the torpedoing. There has never been an adequate explanation for this error in the date on the medal.

Delighted British propagandists struck off and distributed throughout the world tens of thousands of *Lusitania* medals with this legend printed on the box:

> THE "LUSITANIA" MEDAL
> An exact replica of the medal which was designed in Germany and distributed to commemorate the sinking of the "Lusitania."
>
> THIS INDICATES THE TRUE FEELING THE WAR LORDS ENDEAVOUR TO STIMULATE AND IS PROOF POSITIVE THAT SUCH CRIMES ARE NOT MERELY REGARDED FAVOURABLY, BUT ARE GIVEN EVERY ENCOURAGEMENT IN THE LAND OF "KULTUR."
>
> The "Lusitania" was sunk by a German submarine on May 7, 1915. She had on board 1,951 passengers and crew, of whom 1,198 perished.

The British inscription on the box contained one small error —there were 1,959 passengers and crew aboard the ship, not 1,951.

Warship or Passenger Liner?

WAS THE *Lusitania* a warship or a passenger vessel?

There were angry quarrels on this question. According to international law a warship could be attacked on sight. But the sinking of a passenger vessel, even in wartime, was a violation of the law of nations.

The German Foreign Office said that the *Lusitania* was in fact a warship and therefore open to destruction without warning. Had not the *Lusitania* and her sister ship the *Mauretania* been built with funds supplied by the British government at a low rate of interest? And did not the *Lusitania* have emplacements for mounted guns? There was room on the ship for twelve guns with which the *Lusitania* could fire a broadside powerful enough to sink any cruiser afloat. Early in the war, said the Germans, the *Lusitania* had been transferred to the British Admiralty to be used for war purposes.

The Germans had still other arguments. Look in the 1914 edition, they said, of the British register of warships, *Jane's Fighting Ships*, and there you will find a silhouette of the *Lusitania* listed as an "armed merchantman." And Captain Turner of the *Lusitania* was a commander of the British Royal Naval Reserve. He had secret orders, the Germans claimed, to ram any submarine. Finally, said the Germans, when the *Lusitania* sailed from New York on her last voyage, she was armed with four guns of "good size" — two mounted forward and two aft.

The British, placed on the defensive by these charges, dismissed them as plainly false. They answered each charge:

1. All governments, including that of Germany, gave funds to build merchant-marine ships.

2. To say that the *Lusitania* was a warship of the British navy was a rank distortion and falsehood. She was merely a reserve ship, just as every fast ship in the world — including German vessels — was a reserve ship. The *Lusitania* was a passenger ship.

3. It was true that the *Lusitania* was taken over by the Admiralty in the early days of the war but, because of her heavy consumption of coal, she was soon returned to the Cunard Company.

4. The *Lusitania* was, indeed, listed in *Jane's Fighting Ships*, but as a *reserve* ship.

5. It was just a coincidence that Captain Turner was a commander of the British Royal Naval Reserve. But neither the officers nor the crew of the *Lusitania* were regular navy men. What about the German practice in this regard?

6. If German submarines had the right to claim the *Lusitania* as a lawful prize, she had the right to resist them by ramming.

7. The British government denied officially that the *Lusitania* was armed with mounted guns when she left New York on her final trip. This was a plain falsehood, said the British, and they insisted that American records would prove it.

Thus the argument raged. The *Lusitania* case raised a new issue in international law. U-boat warfare brought with it an unexpected problem: Should this novel weapon be discarded in obedience to precedents of international law, or should international law adapt itself to the working of the submarine? Until the *Lusitania* was sunk, whenever an enemy ship was destroyed, the recognized procedure was first to have its passengers saved. The Germans had a right to capture the *Lusitania* if they could, but under the contemporary law of nations the ship could not be sunk without warning and removal of passengers.

Technically, the *Lusitania* was not a warship, despite the German arguments. True, she operated under the direction of the

British Admiralty, but she held a reserve-ship status and she was not officially incorporated into the armed forces as a belligerent ship. All the world knew that the *Lusitania* was a transatlantic liner engaged in the transportation of passengers, freight, and mail. The Americans regarded her as a passenger ship, otherwise she would not have been cleared by the New York port authorities before she sailed on her final voyage. This was made clear in a telegram from Secretary of State Robert Lansing to Ambassador Gerard on June 9, 1915.

The Germans dismissed all these arguments as specious. "The *Lusitania* was a warship and as such deserved her fate! *Schluss*!" ["Finished!"]

Contraband of War?

DID THE *Lusitania* have munitions on board?

The British said no. There were no explosives listed in the manifest, the record of a ship's cargo. But there was a considerable amount of *ammunition*. There were 5,471 cases of cartridges (1,271 cases of unloaded shrapnel shells and 4,200 cases of Remington cartridges for small arms). These were stored on the orlop — a temporary deck below the waterline — and on the lower decks, about 50 yards away from the spot where the torpedo struck.

The British and Germans did not agree on the distinction between *ammunition* and *exploding munitions*. Under a ruling of the United States courts, this part of the *Lusitania*'s cargo did not come under the classification of *munitions* forbidden by American authorities.

The British case was simple: the *Lusitania* carried only cargo of an ordinary kind. There were no *hidden explosives* on board, they said.

The Germans reacted violently. The *Lusitania*, they said, carried explosives and she was, therefore, fair game for German submarines. Any reasonable man could see, they charged, that the *Lusitania* would have remained afloat for hours had it not been for the explosives she carried. The *Lusitania* was equipped with all modern devices to make her unsinkable, yet she went down in eighteen minutes.

And thereon hung a mystery. Was the heat generated by the explosion of one torpedo enough to ignite ten to eleven tons of black powder in the cartridges? Was the second explosion due to the powder in the cartridges? Or to possibly unlisted explosives in the cargo? Or to a bursting boiler? We shall probably never know.

The Germans made still another charge. Several survivors of the *Lusitania* complained that they were suffocated by fumes of gas, perhaps from the torpedo. But Dr. John Braun, a chemist and graduate of the University of Berlin, announced in Pittsburgh a day after the tragedy that the *Lusitania* carried 250,000 pounds of tetrachloride made in Pittsburgh and consigned to the French government to be used in making gas bombs. According to Dr. Braun, the suffocation of the passengers was caused by the escaping tetrachloride, which brought partial asphyxiation. "Evidently," he said, "the German authorities knew what was in the hold of the ship, and it was to their interest to prevent this cargo from reaching its destination."

Dr. Braun became a hero in the German press. Studies of the *Lusitania* case by German scholars include this story. The charge was never proved.

The further contention that the *Lusitania* was carrying Canadian troops was also never substantiated. There was no organized body of troops aboard, although a few reservists may have sailed as ordinary citizens. There were several Canadian families. By no stretch of the imagination could the *Lusitania* be regarded as an army transport and, hence, subject to attack.

The Tragedy Is Investigated

THE LIST of casualties was shocking. According to the Mersey investigation figures (which were not altogether accurate), the passengers were made up of 688 adult males, 440 adult females, 51 male children, 39 female children, and 39 infants.

Of the 688 adult males, 421 were lost and 267 were saved.

Of the 440 adult females, 270 were lost and 170 were saved.

Of the 51 male children, 33 were lost and 18 were saved.

Of the 39 female children, 26 were lost and 13 were saved.

Of the 39 infants, 35 were lost, and 4 were saved.

The crew numbered 702 — 677 men and 25 women.

Of the male members of the crew, 397 were lost and 280 saved.

Of the female members of the crew, 16 were lost and 9 saved.

A total of 1,198 persons perished on the *Lusitania*. Of the Americans on board, 128 were lost and 69 were saved.

The first step after the disaster was the immediate coroner's investigation of the deaths attendant upon the loss of the *Lusitania*. Within three days a coroner's jury returned a verdict at Kinsale, Ireland: "The jury finds that this appalling crime was contrary to international law and the convention of all civilized nations, and we therefore charge the officers of the submarine, and the German Emperor and the government of Germany, under whose orders they acted, with the crime of willful and wholesale murder."

Captain Turner's testimony, in part, at the inquest, was as follows:

Coroner: "Did you receive any special instructions as to the voyage?"

Captain Turner: "Yes, but I am not at liberty to tell what they were."

Coroner: "Did you carry them out?"

Captain Turner: "Yes, to the best of my ability."

Coroner: "Tell us in your own words what happened after passing Fastnet."

Captain Turner: "The weather was clear. We were going at a speed of 18 knots. I was on the port side and heard Second Officer Hefford call out, 'Here's a torpedo.'

"I ran to the other side and saw clearly the wake of a torpedo. Smoke and steam came up between the last two funnels. There was a light shock. Immediately after the first explosion there was another report, but that may possibly have been internal.

"I at once gave the order to lower the boats down to the rails, and I directed that women and children should get into them.

"I also gave orders to stop the ship, but we could not stop as the engines were out of commission. It was not safe to lower boats until the speed was off the vessel.

"When she was struck she listed to starboard. I stood on the bridge when she sank and the *Lusitania* went down under me. She floated about 18 minutes after the torpedo struck her. I was picked up from among the wreckage and afterwards brought aboard a trawler.

"No warship was convoying us. I saw no warship and none was reported to me as having been seen. At the time I was picked up I noticed bodies floating on the surface, but saw no living persons."

Coroner: "Eighteen knots was not the normal speed of the *Lusitania*, was it?"

Captain Turner: "At ordinary times she could make 25 knots, but in wartimes her speed was reduced to 21 knots. My reason for going 18 knots was that I wanted to arrive at Liverpool Bar without stopping and within two or three hours of high waters."

Coroner: "Was a lookout kept for submarines, having regard to previous warnings?"

Captain Turner: "Yes, we had double lookouts."

Coroner: "Were you going a zigzag course at the moment the torpedoing took place?"

Captain Turner: "No, it was bright weather and land was clearly visible."

Coroner: "Was it possible for a submarine to approach without being seen?"

Captain Turner: "Oh, yes, quite possible."

Coroner: "Something has been said regarding the impossibility of launching the boats on the port side."

Captain Turner: "Yes, owing to the listing of the ship."

Coroner: "How many boats were launched safely?"

Captain Turner: "I cannot say."

Coroner: "Were any launched safely?"

Captain Turner: "Yes, and one or two on the port side."

Coroner: "Were your orders promptly carried out?"

Captain Turner: "Yes."

Coroner: "Was there any panic?"

Captain Turner: "No, there was no panic at all. It was almost calm."

Aftermath

THE AMERICAN PUBLIC was outraged by the sinking of the *Lusitania*. The tragedy was responsible to a large extent for bringing the United States and Germany to the verge of war. President Woodrow Wilson protested by diplomatic note several times. On September 1, 1915 — after some quibbling — the German government promised that no passenger ship would be sunk in the future without warning. But on January 8, 1917, the Germans made the fateful decision to renew unrestricted submarine warfare because the war was going badly for them. That decision provoked war with the United States.

The loss of life on the *Lusitania* — 1,198 men, women, and children — was by far the worst among non-warships in World War I. Measured in terms of the millions of lives lost, this amounted to but a few drops in the buckets of blood shed in that conflict. But what set it apart was the fact that the *Lusitania* was the first great transatlantic passenger liner to fall victim to a German submarine. Moreover, the circumstances of the sinking were so dramatic that the entire world took notice of the event. A thousand noncombatant lives lost in land warfare was one thing, but the specter of the drowning children of the *Lusitania* was one not to be erased easily from the memory of a public otherwise hardened to war and its evils. Atrocity, crime, or incident of war — the story of the *Lusitania* remained unforgotten.

As in the case of the *Titanic*, the fate of the *Lusitania* hinged on a combination of "ifs," any one of which, had it been realized, might have saved the gigantic Cunarder from destruction. There might have been no *Lusitania cause célèbre*:

—IF an international tribunal had previously passed on the status of the *Lusitania* as a passenger vessel and IF the Germans had recognized such a decision as authoritative in wartime.

—IF the British had withdrawn the *Lusitania* as a passenger ship and placed her in war service specifically as an armed cruiser.

—IF the British Admiralty had provided the ship with an armed escort—particularly the torpedo boats and destroyers lying at anchor in Queenstown.

—IF the *Lusitania* had not had a fine crossing of the Atlantic, and IF she had been held up even a short time by bad weather.

—IF Captain Schwieger of the *U-20* had made his decision to return to base a few minutes earlier or a few minutes later.

—IF the German U-boat commander had not been seeking prey at the moment the British ship appeared in his periscope lens.

—IF Captain Turner had not reduced the speed of the *Lusitania* at the critical moment.

—IF, instead of bringing his ship near the submarine-infested headlands, Captain Turner had headed instead for mid-channel as he had been instructed to do.

—IF Captain Turner had zigzagged his ship on the final stage of his voyage to Liverpool.

—IF Captain Turner had decided to take a two-point bearing instead of a longer four-point bearing.

Not only the Allies but fate refused to let the Germans forget the sinking of the *Lusitania*. On January 2, 1931, more than fifteen years after the sinking, a bottle was washed up on the shore of Langeness Island, off North Friesland. Covered with mussels and seaweed, it contained a paper on which was written:

LUSITANIA TORPEDOED. WILL SINK WITHIN 10 MINUTES.

This was followed by ten signatures of the ship's passengers with cabin numbers.

The finders forwarded the bottle to the Cunard Company's office in London.

For twenty years the *Lusitania* lay undisturbed off the Irish coast. Then, in 1935, a team of divers who wanted to prove the merits of a new pressure-proof diving suit located the wreck. They found the Cunard liner lying on her side. The next year, according to gossip in the streets of Cobh and Kinsale, an Italian salvage firm tried to reach the *Lusitania* but was driven away by a British naval vessel.

Nothing happened during the next ten years. Then rumors concerning the *Lusitania* were revived. One story was that a British ship had depth-charged the hulk of the sunken liner. In 1950, a rumor flashed through Ireland that a British salvage firm working on the wreck had set off charges placed by a crane on the surface and guided by a diver suspended in a pressure-proof chamber. Four years later another rumor held that a British company had returned to the scene, sent down a diver, set off a charge, and then left after cautioning the crew not to talk.

These rumors aroused the curiosity of a twenty-one-year-old American skin diver, John Light of Boston, who decided to see for himself whether the rumors were true. First he obtained from the Cunard Company a set of plans showing where guns were to be placed on the *Lusitania*. He then got a transcript of the testimony of Gustav Stahl, who had said that he had seen guns on the

Lusitania the day she left New York on her final voyage, and who had been convicted of perjury and sent to prison in 1915. Light came to the conclusion that certain positions described by Stahl were the same as those on the published plans of the ship. He would go down and examine one place just outboard of the children's nursery.

On July 20, 1960, Light went down to 245 feet and operated his underwater camera. He reported that somebody had been at the children's nursery before him. The metal there, he said, showed the effects of recent blasting. A section of the steel deck seemed to have been cut away by torches. Later he added that he had found cables and chains which were not part of the wreck.

In the next three years Light made a total of thirty-eight dives to the *Lusitania*. In 1961, accompanied by another diver, he claimed to have found a long slender object which could have been a gun. The youthful divers insisted that their findings showed that the wreck had been visited before, possibly by British Admiralty divers who had removed the ship's guns. Was it possible, they asked, that President Wilson, his Secretary of State, the Collector of the Port of New York, the Cunard Company, and the British Admiralty were all either wrong or lying in 1915 when they said the *Lusitania* carried no guns? And had Gustav Stahl been wrongly convicted?

Critics called this, "youthful exuberance and an overenthusiastic play for the limelight." On May 1, 1962, newsmen interviewed John Idwal Lewis, seventy-seven, of Stockton, California, the only officer of the *Lusitania* still alive. Here was an eyewitness. Lewis stated that the liner carried no guns or munitions when she was sunk. "I was the third officer at the time and in a position to know. The *Lusitania* didn't have any guns at all to defend itself against a German attack — not even a machine gun on deck. As for munitions, we had a few cases of small arms and revolver bullets below decks — if you want to call them 'munitions.' But we carried them in peacetime, too."

The mystery remains, along with horror of this terrible and seemingly senseless tragedy of modern warfare. Was the sinking of the *Lusitania* justifiable in terms of war, or was it a brutal, wanton act of destruction? This question will probably forever remain unanswered.

Index

(*c*) denotes a crewman of the *Lusitania*;
(*p*) denotes a passenger.